In the Blink of an Eye

In the Blink of an Eye

Dieter Wiesmüller

Walker & Company
New York

The world is full of surprises.
There is something new to discover, wherever you live.
You are never alone, not even for a minute:
in the city or in the country,
in the forest or by the lake,
on the savannah or in the jungle,
during the day or at night—
just look around you!

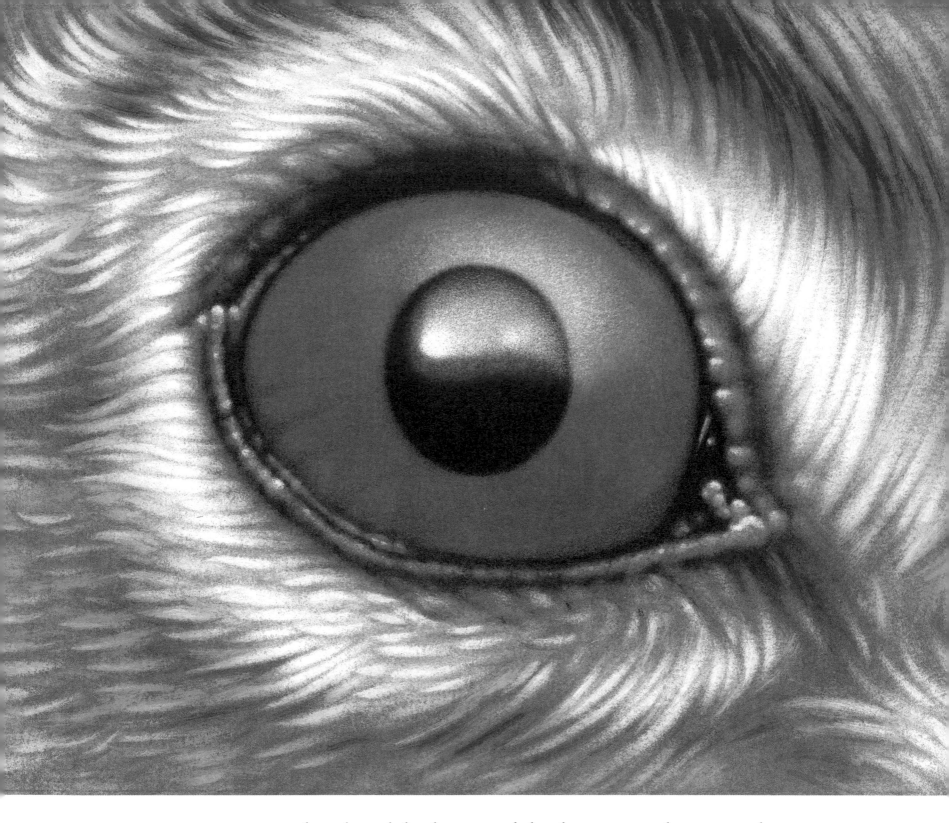

He sits at the edge of the forest with his long ears poking into the sky to catch the sounds from the field. Have you spotted him? He has seen you!

The noisy tractor has frightened him. He hops away, scurrying from side to side. With one last giant leap, he finds safety in his warren.

She perches in her hollow and dreams of the night to come. She hears you pass beneath her tree and awakens from her day of sleep.

As the dusk begins to fall, she soars up into the air. Far above your head, she silently glides through the forest in search of prey.

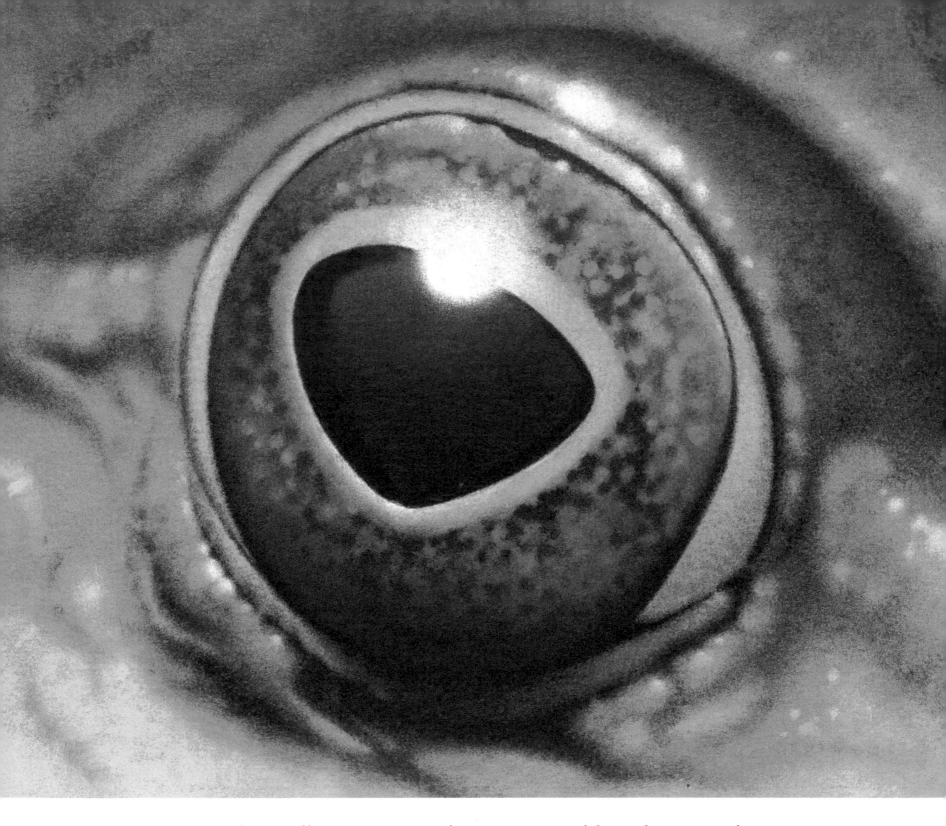

He has endless patience as he squats on a lily pad, waiting for a meal. To you, the hours on the lake crawl by so slowly as you wait for the fish to bite.

Ribbit . . . the little green creature suddenly flicks his tongue to catch a tasty fly. He's caught his meal before you have!

The days are getting shorter. There is a cool breeze in the air.
She knows it is time to fly south to her warm winter home.

Her flock takes wing, following the sun. Soon she is a tiny dot on the horizon. You can still hear her honking in the distance.

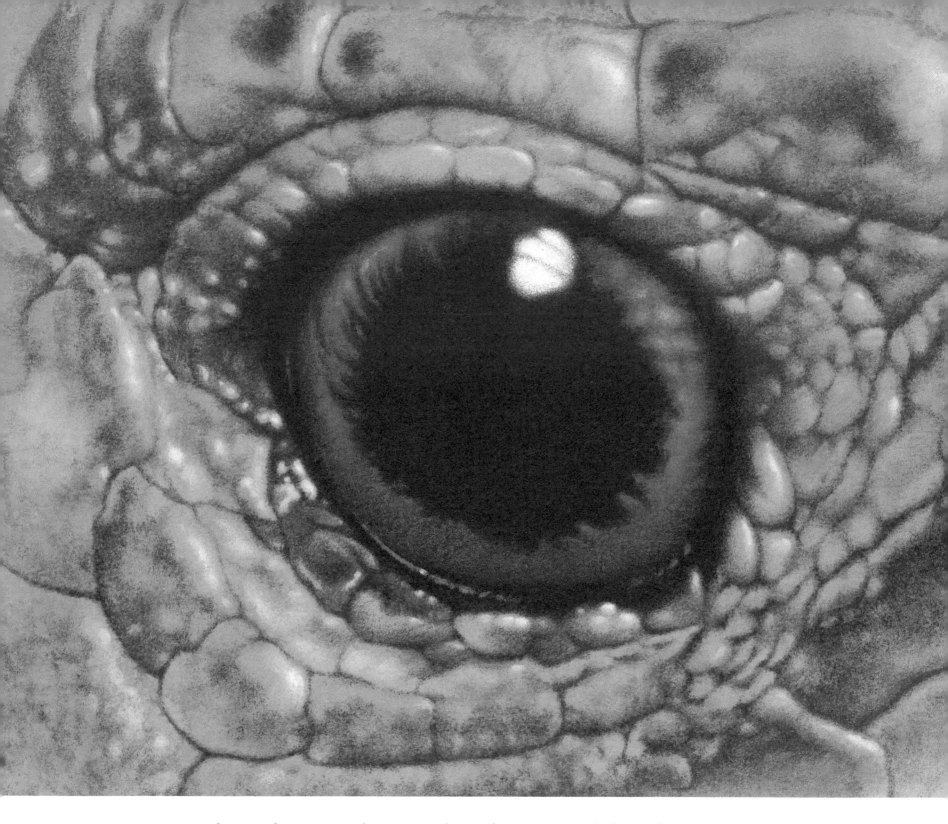

She is drawn to the warmth and wetness of this clearing. Her emerald green scales gleam and glitter as she rests in the moss.

The sound of snapping twigs beneath your feet wakes her from her nap. She quickly vanishes from sight.

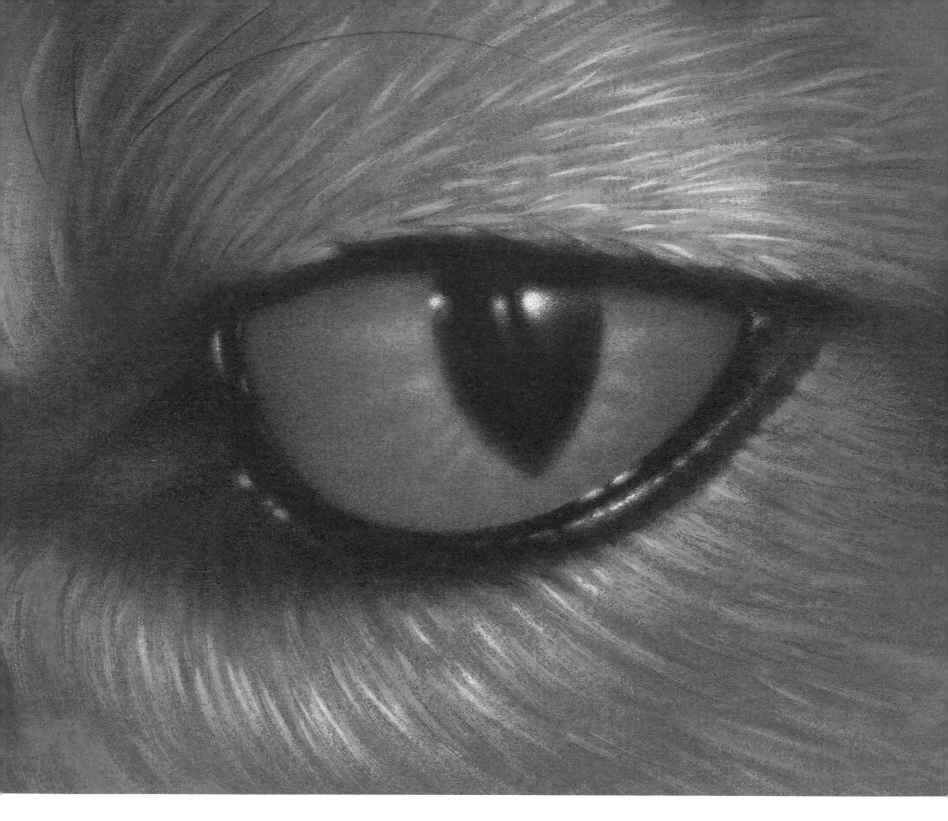

The dogs bark wildly as they follow his scent. They lead the hunting party that is out to get him.

Lured by his gorgeous red pelt and bushy tail, they give chase across meadows, ditches, and fields. Swift and clever, he is able to outrun and outwit them.

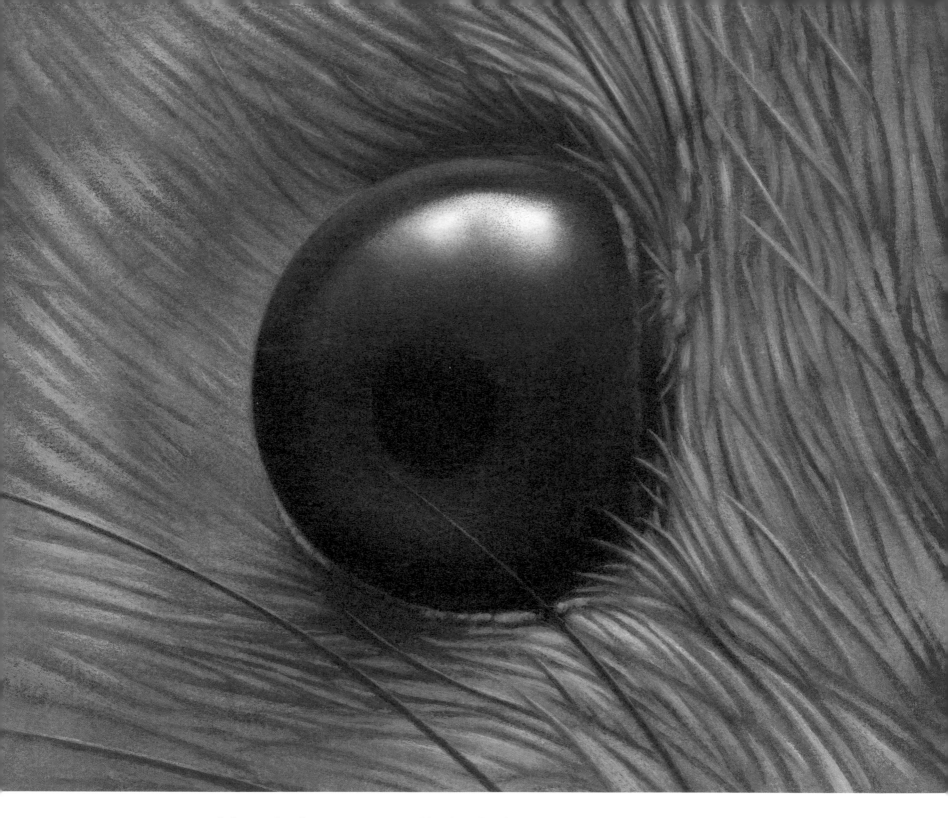

Although she is very small, she feels quite at home in this soaring cathedral. Sitting in her corner, she hungrily nibbles a crumb.

You don't even hear her quiet rustling as you walk down the aisle.
Startled when you come too near, she anxiously scurries off.

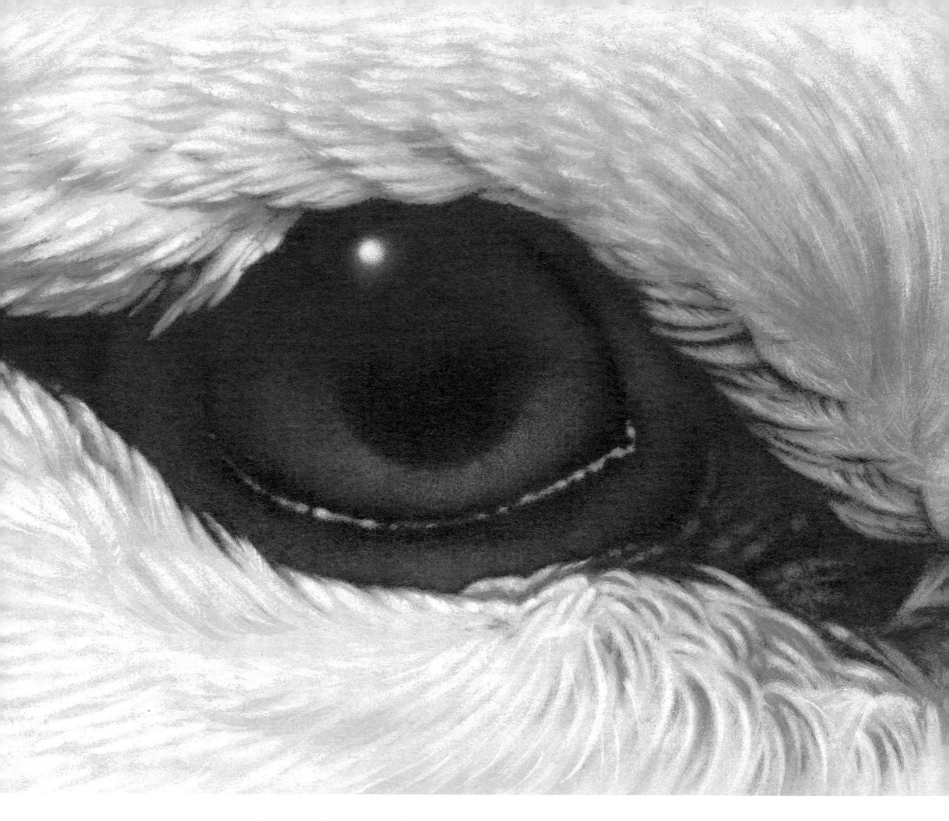

From his rooftop nest he sees you coming and going. But do you notice when he leaves for the winter?

You may think he's off delivering babies, but he's only migrated south. He'll be back next spring, since he returns to the same nest every year.

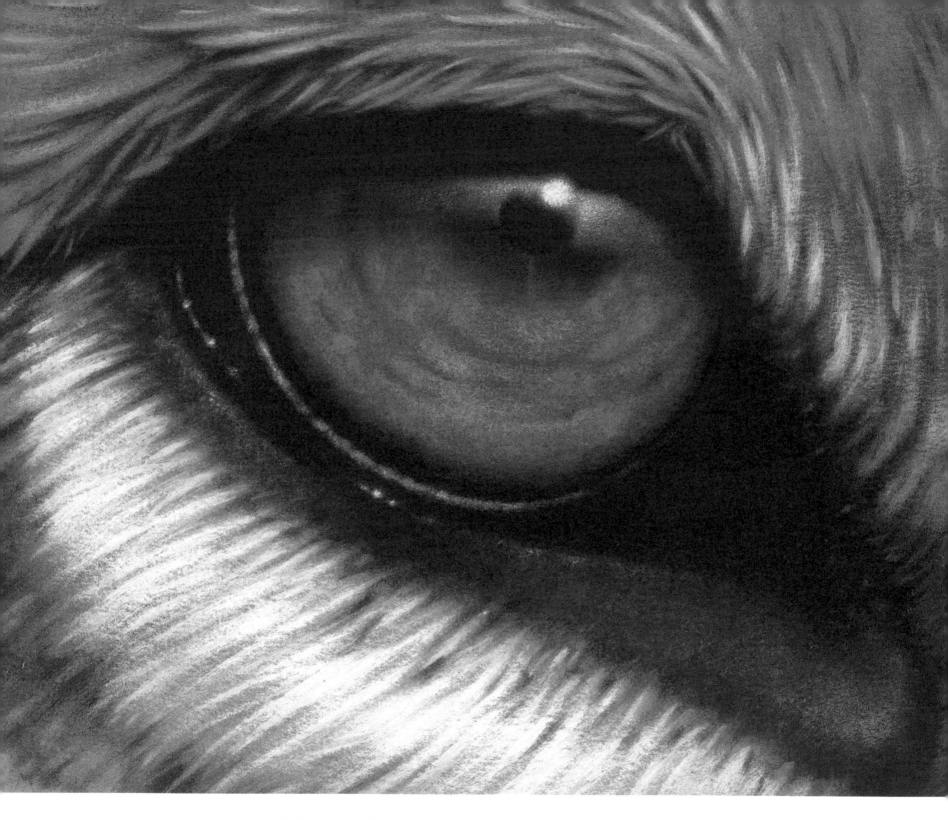

His powerful roar echoes across the savannah as he rests majestically
in the shade of his favorite tree.

He will put up with being photographed. But you had better keep your distance. This kingly cat doesn't welcome visitors to his lair.

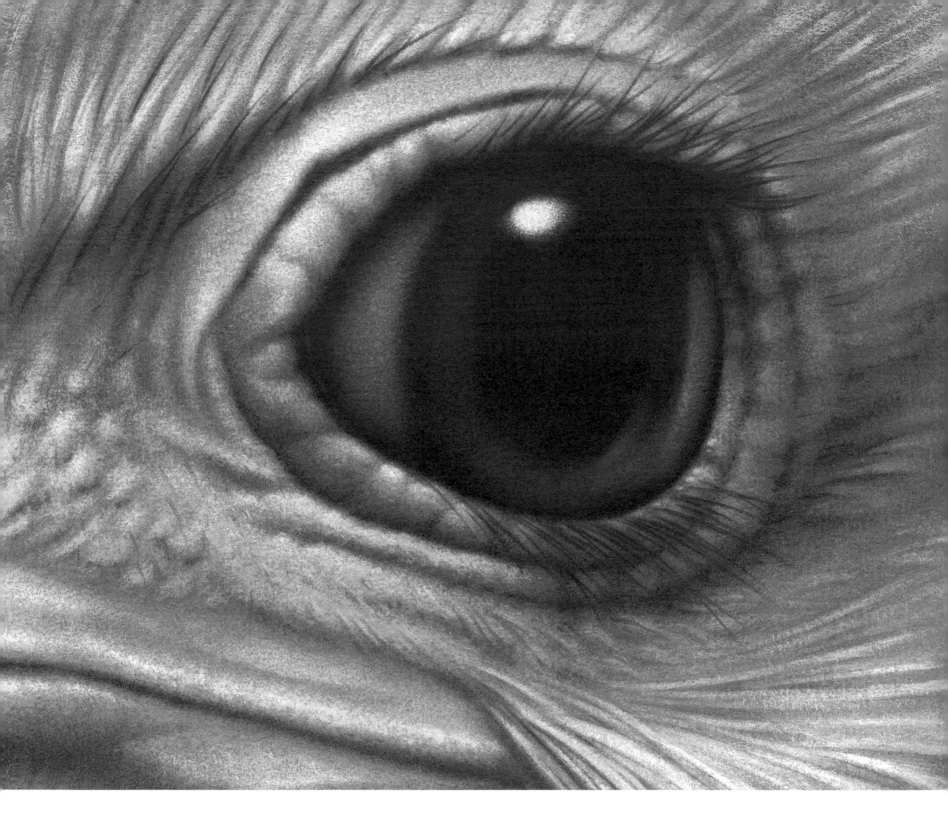

What is this enormous bird doing outside your village again? He
cannot fly, so maybe you can chase him down.

With his large, powerful legs, he will be difficult to outrun. With long, springy strides, he wheels around and struts back to his clutch of eggs.

As you travel through the rain forest, the green curtain of plants and vines hides the amber eyes that watch your every move.

His spotted fur is an excellent camouflage when he prowls through the jungle. Now, resting on a tree branch after eating his fill, he lazily flexes his muscles.

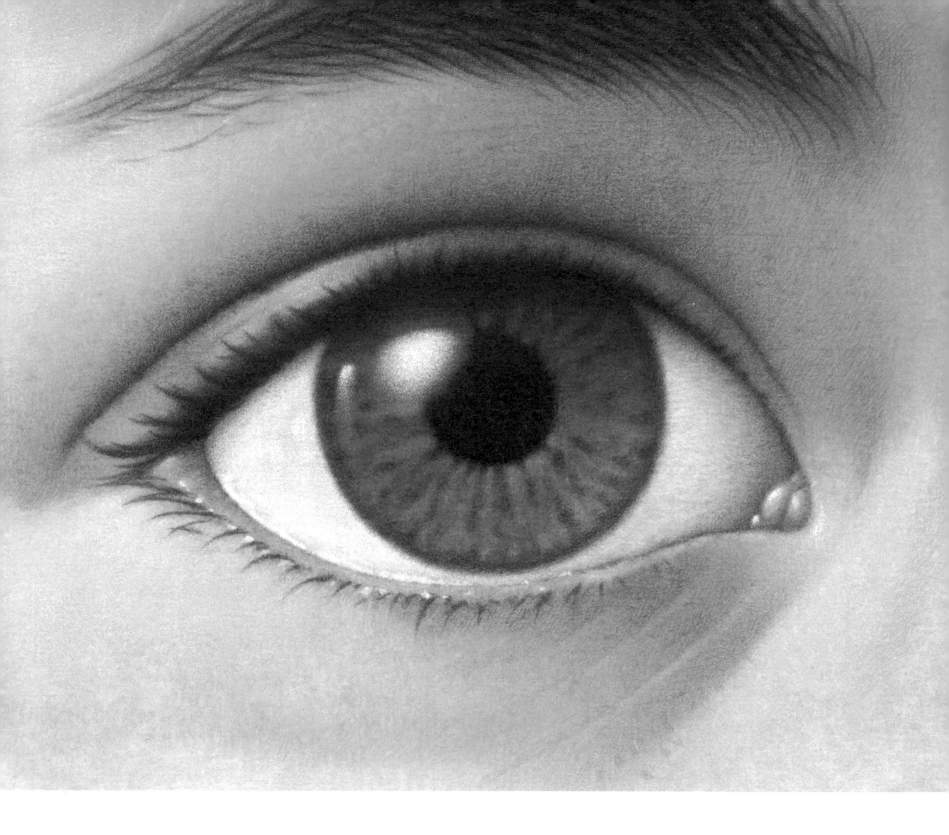

You walk through the world, master of all you see, but don't be blind to the bounty around you.

Wherever you go, remember you are not alone. Learn to see the creatures that share your world.

Animals in This Book

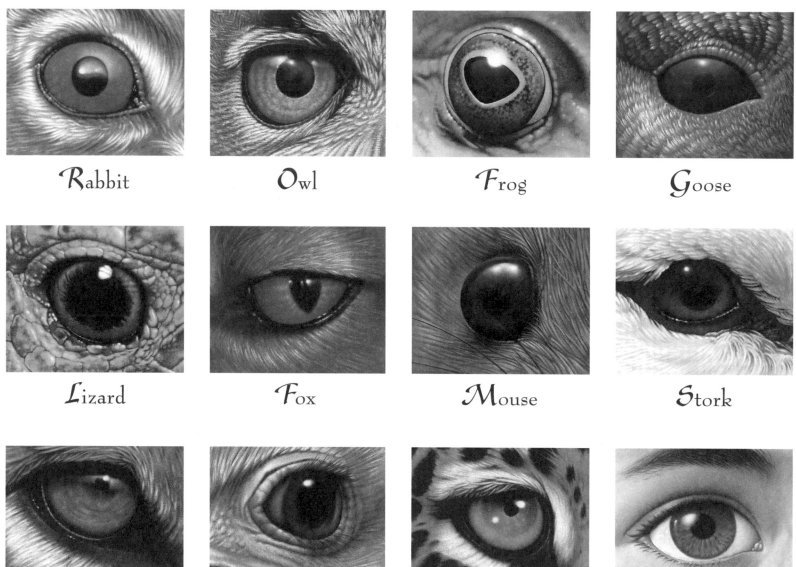

Rabbit

Owl

Frog

Goose

Lizard

Fox

Mouse

Stork

Lion

Ostrich

Leopard

Human

Originally published in German under the title *Augenblick*; first published in the United States of America in 2002 by Walker Publishing Company, Inc.

Published simultaneously in Canada by Fitzhenry and Whiteside, Markham, Ontario L3R 4T8

For information about permission to reproduce selections from this book, write to Permissions, Walker & Company, 435 Hudson Street, New York, New York 10014

Library of Congress Cataloging-in-Publication Data
available upon request
ISBN 0-8027-8854-8 (hardcover)
ISBN 0-8027-8855-6 (reinforced)

The artist used a mixture of transparent and opaque tempera paint to create the illustrations for this book.

Book design by Karen Kollmetz
Type design by Victoria Allen

Visit Walker & Company's Web site at www.walkerbooks.com

Printed in Germany

10 9 8 7 6 5 4 3 2 1